537

ELECTRICITY and MAGNETISM

What's in the book

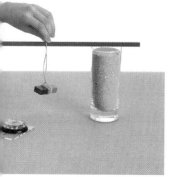

What are magnets?

Have you ever used a magnet? You cannot see why it works, but you can see how the magnet pulls small pieces of iron or steel towards it. This power to **attract** metal is called **magnetism**.

▶ Most magnets are made from iron or steel. Magnets come in many shapes and sizes. Look at the bar magnets and horseshoe magnets in the photograph. Magnets can also be shaped like cylinders or rings.

◀ This hiker is using her magnetic compass to find way through the mounta The needle of the compa is a magnet. It will alway point to the north. A hik can use this to keep a se of his or her direction.

FastFact
The device used to detect and measure magnetism is called a magnetometer.

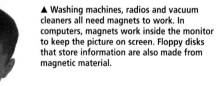

▲ Washing machines, radios and vacuum cleaners all need magnets to work. In computers, magnets work inside the monitor to keep the picture on screen. Floppy disks that store information are also made from magnetic material.

◄ Collect objects from around the house and try to guess which ones a magnet will pick up. Then test them with your magnet. Were you surprised?

Push or pull

Every magnet has two strongly magnetic areas called **poles**. On a bar magnet the poles are at opposite ends. Find the poles on your magnet. How many pins can you hang from different places on the magnet?

▲ Just like the Earth, a magnet has a north pole and a south pole. Push the ends of two magnets together. Do their poles attract each other? Do they push apart or repel? Try turning one of the magnets around. Now what happens?

▶ Put magnets on some toy trains and cars. Some will repel, or race away, from each other.

◀ This experiment shows how to make a magnet float in the air. Find two round or bar-shaped magnets. Fix one into a thick layer of modelling clay, then make a fence around it out of pencils. Now lower the second magnet above the first, north poles together. What happens when you let go?

FastFact
The Earth's magnetic poles extend for thousands of kilometres into space.

▲ This train has no wheels. It glides along on air. The train is a maglev – short for magnetic levitation, which means floating on magnets. The magnetism in the rails repels the bottom surface of the train, allowing it to float along.

North and south

A **magnetic compass** can help you travel in the right direction when you do not know the way. Compasses have been used for many centuries to help people **navigate** on land and sea. The very first compasses were pieces of magnetic stone hung on threads. Long ago, people knew that when magnets hang freely they always swing to the north.

▼ Fill two tumblers with sand and place a pencil across them. Hang a bar magnet from the pencil with thread. Check which way the magnet points using a compass. Label the north-pointing pole on the magnet 'north' and the other pole 'south'.

FastFact
Legend has it that the first magnet was discovered by a shepherd when the iron tip of his crook stuck to a lodestone.

After many years, scientists found that Earth itself acts like a huge magnet. e pole, called the magnetic north pole, is nd in the far north. The magnetic south le lies in the far south. The north pole of ordinary magnet is attracted to the rth's magnetic north pole. The magnetic es shift position slightly from year to ar. They are not exactly the same as the rth Pole and South Pole, which are two ed geographical places.

◀ This experiment helps you find where north lies. Magnetise a needle (see page 13), then tape it to the top of a cork. If you can find one, use a flat cork. Float the cork in a dish of water. Now watch as the needle swings to point in one direction, and turns the cork. Use a magnetic compass to check which end of the needle is pointing north. Now label the north and south poles of the needle with a blob of paint on the cork next to each end of the needle.

The Earth's magnetic ld traps tiny particles velling through space m the Sun. As these rticles enter the Earth's nosphere above the rth and South Poles, the r begins to glow and trange curtain of light pears. These ghostly, ncing lights are known the aurora.

Magnetic attraction

Can a magnet's power work through different materials? Try picking up a pin through thin pieces of cloth, paper, plastic or rubber. Is the magnetic **force** weaker?

▶ Have a magnetic fishing contest. Cut out some bright fish shapes and attach a paper clip to each one. Put the fish in a bowl. Tie a magnet to the end of a piece of string on a stick. Can you catch fish through the side of the bowl?

◀ Draw a dinosaur on a piece of cardboard and scatter a handful of pins on the top. Now move a magnet around underneath the cardboard. You can use the force of the magnet to arrange the pins in all sorts of patterns on the dinosaur's body.

▲ Make a paper acrobat and tape a needle to the back. Feed some thread through the needle, then stretch it taut between two chairs. Find a position where the magnet can keep the needle trembling upright, and make the acrobat dance.

Make or break

It is easy to make a magnet but, although it seems strong, its power can easily be taken away.

Magnets can harm audio or video apparatus. See for yourself by dragging a magnet over an unwanted audio cassette **tape**. Now play the tape. The magnet has upset the magnetic sound pattern on the tape ribbon.

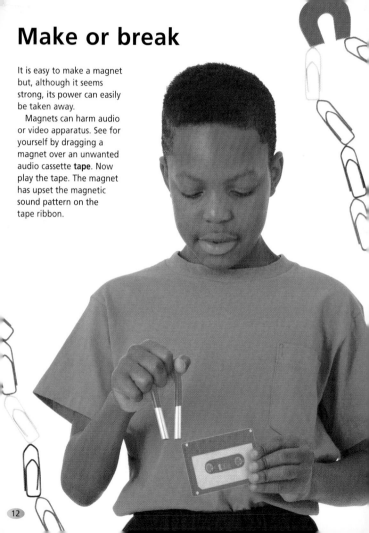

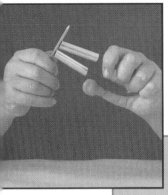

◀ Make your own magnet. Stroke a nail with a magnet about 50 times. Always stroke with the same pole, in the same direction. Does the magnet grow more powerful with each stroke?

Make long chains of paper [clip]s with a strong magnet. [Eac]h clip attracts the next. [Do]es a chain lose its [ma]gnetism if you pull it [off] the magnet?

Magnetise a steel nail and [not]e how many pins it can [pic]k up. Now tap the nail [aga]inst a table five times. [Ho]w many pins can it pick [up] now?

Fields of force

The power of a magnet to push and pull is invisible. It works around a magnet in an area called the **magnetic field**. A magnet cannot attract outside this field of power.

▶ See a magnetic field for yourself! Place two bar magnets under a sheet of paper, like poles facing (north to north, or south to south). Sprinkle iron filings on the paper. The filings arrange themselves in a pattern of curved lines.

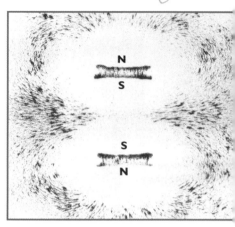

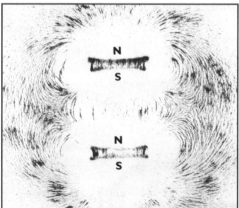

◀ The patterns of lines that are picked out by the filings are called lines of force. Can you see where the lines are closest together?

Repeat the experiment, this time with the north pole of one magnet facing the south pole of the other. The magnets must not touch. How has the magnetic field changed?

◀ Migrating birds use the Sun and stars to help them find their way. So how do they manage to stay on course on cloudy days? Scientists believe birds can sense the Earth's magnetic field and use it as a guide.

Horseshoe magnets usually have a keeper to protect them. Put some paper clips in front of a horseshoe magnet. Now put the keeper in place and try again. Does the keeper make the magnetic field change?

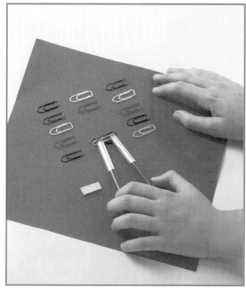

What causes electricity and magnetism?

Everything that exists – including your body – is made from microscopic particles, called **atoms**. The atoms themselves are made up of even smaller particles called **protons**, **neutrons** and **electrons**. It is the electrons that create both electricity and magnetism.

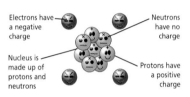

Electrons have a negative charge

Neutrons have no charge

Nucleus is made up of protons and neutrons

Protons have a positive charge

▲ Atom consisting of a nucleus of protons and neutrons, surrounded by electrons.

Atomic structure

Atoms, the building blocks of everything that exists in the universe, are extremely tiny. In the middle of an atom is a **nucleus** made of two **subatomic particles** called protons and neutrons. Spinning around the nucleus are even smaller particles called electrons. Electrons have a negative electrical charge, protons have a positive electrical charge, while neutrons have no charge and are electrically neutral, which is how they got their name.

Charged atoms

Usually an atom has the same number of electrons and protons, so the positive and negative electrical charges cancel each other

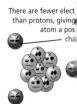

There are fewer elect than protons, giving atom a pos cha

▶ A positively charged atom

out. If an atom loses an electron, the positive charges outnumber the negative ones, so the atom becomes positively charg Likewise, if an atom gains an electron it becomes negatively charged. A charged atom is called an **ion**. It is this losing and gaining of electrons that causes electricity

How electricity is created

Electricity is created by a flow of electron jumping from one atom to another, givin them an electric charge. This also explains why some materials **conduct** electricity an others do not. The atoms in some materia such as silver, **aluminium** and copper, will lose at least one of their electrons quite easily, allowing electricity to flow along them. In other materials, such as rubber a wood, the atoms hang on tightly to all th electrons. If electrons cannot jump from c atom to another, electricity cannot flow. kind of substance is called an **insulator**.

▲ Electrons jump from one atom to anoth thereby creating a flow of electricity.

Magnetic field

As well as causing electricity, electrons are responsible for magnetism. Electrons are constantly spinning around the nucleus of an atom. In most atoms, each electron spins in a different direction. But in some substances, such as **iron** and **nickel**, the electrons in each atom spin the same way, creating a **magnetic field** around the atom.

A magnetic material is composed of lots of small areas called **domains**. A domain is a tiny region of magnetism inside a magnetic substance in which the atoms line up in the same direction to form two magnetic poles. Normally, the poles of different domains point in different directions, so their magnetic fields cancel each other out and the substance is not magnetic. To turn the substance into a magnet, the domains must be made to face the same way.

◀ In most atoms electrons spin in different directions around the nucleus, and the atom has no magnetic field.

▶ The electrons in a piece of iron spin in the same direction around the nucleus, and create a magnetic field.

How magnetism is created and destroyed

By stroking a piece of iron in one direction with a magnet, the magnetic domains are all pulled around to face the same way. Now, the magnetic fields of the domains don't cancel each other out. In fact, the combined magnetic fields of all the domains put together turns the piece of iron into a magnet!

As easily as you can make magnets, you can also destroy them. By hitting the magnet with a hammer, the domains are knocked out of alignment. The magnetic fields now cancel each other out and the magnet loses its magnetism.

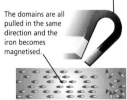

A magnet is stroked across the piece of iron, thereby aligning the domains.

The magnetic domains within the iron are all mixed up so that their north and south poles cancel each other out.

The domains are all pulled in the same direction and the iron becomes magnetised.

By striking the magnetized iron with a hammer, the domains lose their alignment and the iron loses it magnetism.

Unmagnetised piece of iron

▲ **Magnetised piece of iron**

◀ **Demagnetised piece of iron**

Power base

Electricity helps people at home and at work. In factories, forklift trucks lift heavy loads, while robots assemble cars. Electric furnaces melt metals and bake clay into bricks. In offices, fax machines, photocopiers and computers save time and effort.

▶ How many types of electrical equipment can you find in your home?

◀ A fairground Ferris wheel uses electricity to spin its riders. Most forms of transport now use electricity. Electric trains and trams carry people to and from work in cities. Motor vehicles use electric sparks to explode the gasoline that runs their engines. Diesel electric engines power many boats and ships. Vessels and aeroplanes are navigated by means of electronic instruments. Many of the special controls in space vehicles run on electricity.

A city never shuts down
the night. In the
ning, many people go
to theatres, eat in
taurants or attend
odlit football games.
ffic moves through the
and the street lights
ne all night. Without
tricity, these activities
uld stop at sundown.

◀ Animals also use electricity. A fish called
the electric eel can produce up to 500 volts
of electricity using special organs in its
body. Eels use electricity for self-defence
and to catch prey. An electric shock from an
eel is enough to stun a large animal! Eels
also use electricity to sense objects around
them so that they do not bump into things
in murky water.

FastFact
Doctors in 100 AD advised
patients to bathe with an
electric eel to ease pain
in their joints.

Fantastic static

You can make electricity just by rubbing objects against each other. Rubbing makes **static electricity**, which can pull things together or push them apart.

▼ Rub a balloon on your sweater, then ho it over your head. The balloon is surround by an electric field, rather like a magnetic field. It's hair-raising!

◀ Charge a balloon with static electricity, then hold it next to a thin stream of water. As if by magic, the water bends towards the balloon. How far can you make the stream bend? The electric field around the balloon pulls things towards it.

Cut up some coloured card and stick it [tog]ether to make some paper bugs. Put [the]m in a shallow box with a clear plastic [lid.] Rub the lid with a dust rag. The bugs [jum]p up and stick to the lid. Move your [fin]ger over them to make the bugs dance.

▲ You can see static electricity in a thunderstorm. Lightning is a giant spark of static electricity that has built up in thunder clouds. It can jump between clouds or down to Earth. After a flash of lightning, count the seconds until the thunder. Divide by five and this will tell you how many kilometres away the storm is.

Store it up

The electricity we use at home is not like **static electricity**. It flows along wires. The electricity is created by particles called **electrons**. Electrons move along a wire like beads moving down a tube. This creates the flow of electricity, or the **electric current**. The wire leads, or conducts electricity to where it is needed.

FastFact
In 1799 Alessandro Volta invented the battery.

In 1820, a Danish professor named Hans Christian Oersted was giving a lecture. He happened to drop a wire carrying electricity across a **magnetic compass**. As he picked up the wire, he saw that the compass needle had swung out of place, and was no longer pointing north. Oersted was the first to notice that wires carrying electricity have a **magnetic field**.

◀ Later on in the 19th century, a famous scientist called Michael Faraday found that if he moved a magnet in and out of a coil of wire, an electric current would flow through the wire. He could now produce, or generate, electricity. Today, all our power stations still use Faraday's method of producing electricity.

▶ Batteries come in all shapes and sizes: from tiny batteries for cameras to large ones for cars and trucks. What do you use batteries for?

◀ You can make a battery with an iron key, a copper coin, blotting paper and vinegar. Clean the coin and the key with sandpaper. Dip a small square of the blotting paper in vinegar and place it between the coin and key. Now wrap wire around a compass 10 times. Hold one end of the wire to the key, the other to the coin. The current in the wire will affect the needle of the magnetic compass.

Batteries store chemicals that react together to push electrons along a wire. When the chemicals are used up, the battery becomes 'flat'. Which of your toys use batteries?

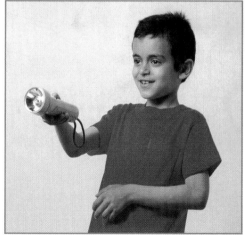

Let there be light

bulb holders

insulated wire

crocodile clips

2.5v or 3.5v flashlight bulbs with screw fittings

1.5v batteries (battery strength is measured in volts, or v for short)

double or single battery holder

▶ Electricity needs a path to flow along. Connecting a wire from each terminal on a battery to each terminal on a bulb holder will make a circuit and light the bulb. Use insulating tape to fix wires from a bulb holder, one to each end of a single battery. Is there a difference if you swap the wires on the terminals of the battery?

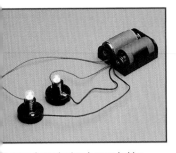

Put two batteries in a battery holder. The batteries must be put in the right way around. Use two wires to join two bulbs directly to the battery holder. This arrangement is called a parallel circuit. Try unscrewing one bulb. What happens to the circuit? Why?

Now make a series circuit, where only one wire is attached to each terminal of the battery holder and another runs between one bulb and the other. Both bulbs are on one circuit. What happens to this circuit if you unscrew a bulb?

Was there a change in the brightness of the bulbs when you tried the parallel and series circuits? What difference did it make, using one or two batteries?

▼ Make a light-up frog. Draw a frog on one side of some folded cardboard. Use a pencil to make holes in the cardboard where the eyes should be. Remove the bulbs from your parallel circuit and tuck the rest of the circuit inside the frog. Screw the bulbs through the holes in the cardboard into the bulb holders behind. Ask an adult to make holes in two ping-pong balls, then place them over the bulbs. Connect the wires to the battery and watch the eyes light up!

Conductors

Materials that let **electric current** flow through them are known as **conductors**. Electricity cannot pass through other materials, called **insulators**. These materials stop currents flowing where they could be dangerous.

Vrap two strips of
lboard in silver foil to
ke a switch – foil
ducts current. Clip them
a circuit. Bring the
er tips together and the
lights up. Each time
switch off a light, you
ak the circuit. Switch it
and the circuit is
nplete again.

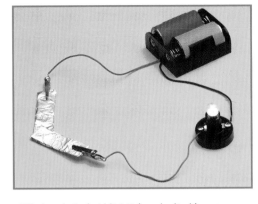

◄ What conducts electricity? Make a circuit with a gap
between crocodile clips. Put objects between the clips.
The current is flowing if the bulb lights up. What do
conductors have in common?

▲ A burglar sets off an alarm by touching
part of a security system with his foot. His
touch closes a circuit, and may trigger an
alarm bell, flashing lights and even an alarm
at the local police station.

Electromagnets

An **electromagnet** is a magnet that is powered by electricity. A simple electromagnet consists of a coil of wire wrapped around an **iron** bar. It becomes a magnet when an **electric current** flows through the wire.

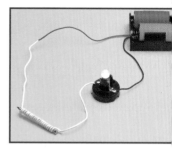

▲ To make an electromagnet, make this circuit using insulated wire and a steel or iron nail. You could include a bulb to help stop the wire from getting hot. How many paper clips can your electromagnet lift? Try changing the strength of the magnet by winding more wire around the nail, or using a different number of batteries.

▲ Electromagnets are used to pick out magnetic metals from piles of scrap for recycling. A crane lifts the electromagnet with metal stuck to it. When the electricity is cut off, it drops its load.

Make an electromagnetic truck! Cut up a ‪cardboard‬ box to make the body of a truck ‪and‬ use the rest of it to make the arm of a ‪crane‬. Cut slits in the back of the truck to ‪push‬ the arm through. Push a pencil through ‪the‬ sides of the lorry and then through a ‪the‬ thread spool.

▲ Wind wire around a nail about 30 times. Thread the loose ends of wire through the free end of the crane, down the arms and over the spool. Behind the spool, connect the wires to a battery. What can your truck pick up? Disconnect the wires when the truck is not in use to save the battery.

Power sources

The electricity we use at home is made in power stations. Most burn coal, oil or use **nuclear fuel** to make heat.

▶ In a coal-fired power station, burning coal heats water to make steam. The steam spins the blades of a machine called a turbine. This turns a large magnet inside coils of wire, which generates electricity.

◀ Burning fuels can pollute the Earth's atmosphere. Other ways of making electricity include using the force of falling water to spin turbines in hydroelectric power stations or using moving air in wind generators. Electricity is sent around the country along a network of wires held up by steel towers called pylons. In towns and cities, the electricity flows along underground cables. Electricity is reduced to a lower voltage by a transformer before it enters buildings.

FastFact
Most power stations generate an alternating current (a.c.) of electricity, rather than a direct current (d.c.).

◄ Make a pinwheel to see the power of moving air. Cut a square out of thin cardboard. Using a ruler, make a mark at 1cm to the right of each corner. Cut a straight line from each mark to 1cm away from the centre. In turn, bend the squared-off end of each flap into the centre. Now ask an adult to attach the pinwheel to a stick or pencil with a long pin, so it can spin freely.

▲ Solar cells can change sunlight directly into electricity. Large panels of solar cells can use the Sun's energy to power satellites that orbit the Earth.

Power up

The electricity that we use in our homes, schools, offices and factories will most likely have been **generated** by a power station. Most power stations create electricity by burning fossil fuels such as coal, oil or natural gas. Fossil fuels are made deep within the Earth from the remains of prehistoric plants and animals. Once the electricity has been generated it is transmitted along cables to transformer stations, transmission substations and distribution substations where the voltage is adjusted to reach the correct voltage for all the different users.

2. Step-up transformer

A typical power station generates about [?] million kilowatts of electricity at 25,000 vo[?] The step-up transformer boosts the voltag[?] to 765,000 volts before the electricity is transmitted around the country.

1. Power station

Inside the power station fuel is burnt in a combustion chamber. The heat released turns water into steam. The steam is forced through a machine called a **turbine**, making the turbine blades spin. The turbine is connected to a generator, inside which is a powerful magnet surrounded by a coil of wire. As the blades of the turbine rotate, they make the magnet spin inside the coil of wire, producing electricity.

High-voltage electricity is delivered directly from the distribution substation to heavy industries, such as car and steel factories.

WARNING: Never try to climb into a substation. High voltage sparks can 'jump' off equipment, so you don't even need to touch something to be **electrocuted**.

8. Home

Electricity has all sorts of uses in the home. It provides lighting and powers lots of useful appliances, such as radios, TVs and air conditioners. All these devices run on small electric motors, which convert the electrici[?] into mechanical power. The heating in many houses also runs on electrici[?]

3. Pylons
Pylons support the overhead transmission lines that transmit the electricity produced in the power station throughout the country.

Power stations are not the only things that produce electricity. **Static electricity** builds up when particles of water and ice bump into each other inside a cloud. This electrical charge is released as lightning.

4. Subtransmission substation
Here, a step-down transformer reduces the voltage of the electricity from 138,000 volts to 12,500 volts.

5. Distribution substation
Here, the voltage of the electricity is reduced from 34,500 volts to 2,000 volts for use in industry.

WARNING: Never fly a kite near overhead power lines! If the kite touches the cables you will be electrocuted.

6. Another distribution substation.
Here, the voltage of the electricity may be further reduced for use in shopping centres, schools, and hospitals.

WARNING: Never seek shelter from a thunderstorm under a tree. If lightning strikes it will hit the tallest object around which often makes trees a target.

lectricity pole
istribution transformer on the electricity pole uces the voltage of the electricity to 220 volts 20 volts for use in homes, stores and offices.

Glossary

Aluminium is an element which is light, silvery and bends and changes shape easily.

The **atmosphere** is a layer of gases that surrounds the Earth.

Atoms are microscopic particles that form the building blocks of everything that exists in the universe.

To **attract** is to pull something with an invisible power. Magnets attract objects made of iron or steel.

Batteries store chemicals that make electricity by pushing electrons along a wire.

Cables are heavy, insulated wires, used to carry electricity.

A **circuit** is a path followed by an electric current. A gap in a circuit breaks the path so that the current no longer flows.

Conductors are materials through which electricity is able to flow.

A **domain** is a small region of magnetism in a magnetic material.

Electrical charge is the movement of electricity along a conductor.

An **electric current** is a flow of electrons through a wire or other conductor.

An **electric field** is the area around an object where its electric charge has the power to pull things towards it or push them away.

Electricity is a form of energy used to make light and heat and to run machiner

An **electromagnet** is made from a coi wire wrapped around an iron bar. Wh electric current flows through the wir it becomes a magnet.

Electric shock happens when electrici passes through your body, for examp if you touch an electric circuit. It is extremely dangerous and can kill you

Electric wall socket is the outlet in the walls of your home that allows household appliances to be plugged in to the house's electrical supply.

Electrons are tiny particles in atoms which carry electricity and cause magnetism.

ctrocuted is when someone is filled **th** electricity, which is very dangerous. ctrocution can cause severe burns or en death and electricity should be ated with caution.

ppy disks are coated with magnetic terial. They are used to store ormation.

ce is energy that changes the shape motion of something.

generate electricity is to produce it. tricity is produced by generators.

droelectric power stations use ter to turn turbines and produce tricity.

lated wire is wire which is coated in stic. Electricity cannot flow through terials that are insulators.

lators are materials through which tricity is unable to flow.

s are charged atoms.

i is one of the elements and the most ely used of all the metals.

eper is a piece of metal placed on end of a magnet that helps to stop om demagnetising by keeping the ains in aligmnet.

Like poles repel each other; unlike poles attract each other.

Lines of force are the lines around a magnet that show the magnetic field.

A **magnetic compass** is used by travellers to find their way. It has a moving needle that always points north.

A **magnetic field** is the area around a magnet that attracts or repels magnetic material with magnetic properties.

Magnetism is the way a magnet attracts objects made of certain metals.

Migrating animals travel to warmer parts of the world before winter.

Navigating is using various means, such as compasses, the Sun and road maps, to find your way from one destination to another.

Negatively charged atoms have an extra electron so the negative charges outnumber the positive ones.

Neutrons are tiny particles which do not contain an electrical charge and which help to make up the nucleus of an atom.

Nickel is an element which is white, magnetic and bends and changes shape easily.

North Pole and **South Pole** are the names the most northerly and southerly points o the Earth's surface. The North and South Poles are different to the Earth's magnetic north and south poles, which are where t Earth's magnetic fields are strongest.

Nuclear fuel is material, such as urani or plutonium, consumed to produce nuclear energy.

The **nucleus** is the central part of all atoms and is composed of protons an neutrons.

Parallel means running alongside something. Railway tracks are a good example of parallel lines.

Poles are the places on a magnet where t magnetic field is strongest.

Positively charged atoms have an extra neutron so the positive charges outnumber the negative ones.

Protons are tiny particles which contain a positive electrical charge and which help to make up the nucle of an atom.

Pylons are tall towers made of steel girders. They hold cables carrying electricity high above the ground.

To **repel** is to push away. Similar pole magnets repel each other.

lar cells are made of thin layers of a rd, shiny material called silicon. The n convert sunlight into electricity.

tic electricity is produced when tw ulating materials are rubbed gether.

subatomic particle is a particle that aller than an atom and one that lps to make up an atom.

pe (magnetic tape) is a narrow leng plastic coated with a magnetic terial. It can be used to record visu dio or computer information.

erminal is one end of a battery. Eac ttery has two terminals. A circuit ist run between them for electricity flow.

ransformer can convert high voltag ctricity from the national grid into ver voltage electricity.

urbine is like a large fan that is ned by steam or running water. It ns a magnet within coils of wire to ke electricity.

ts are a measurement of ctrical force.

nd generators are similar to ndmills and use the wind's power to duce electricity.

Lab book

Conductors vs. Magnetic Materials

Conduct experiments with a magnet and the electric circuit you can make following the instructions on pages 24–27. Keep the chart handy in case anyone tests you!

Put a tick or a cross in each of the boxes as you test the different materials

Name of material	Does it conduct?	Is it magnetic?
Chalk		
Wood		
Glass		
Gold		
Cork		
Lead		
Rubber		
Meteorite		
Steel		

Name of material	Does it conduct?	Is it magnetic?
Plastic		
Paper		
Copper		
Iron		
China		
Aluminium		
Silver		
Ice		
Nickel		
Lodestone		
Amber		
Iron magnet		
Diamond		
Coral		
Brass		

Design your own electrically powered machine

Questions and answers

Test your knowledge of electricity and magnetism with this multiple choice quiz.

Which of these substances is magnetic?
A. Gold
B. Iron
C. Aluminium

What would happen if you put the north pole of one magnet next to the north pole of another one?
A. The magnets would stick together
B. The magnets would move apart
C. Nothing

Which of these substances is an insulator?
A. Rubber
B. Gold
C. Steel

What is shown in the photograph below?
A. Atmosphere
B. Aurora
C. North Pole

What is an insulator?
A. A substance that is not magnetic
B. A substance that does not conduct electricity
C. A magnetic substance that conducts electricity

What is a natural source of static electricity?
A. Lightning
B. Sunlight
C. Lodestones

What are the two types of electricity called?
A. Conducting and insulating
B. Current and static
C. Battery and mains

What does a keeper do?
A. Stops a magnet losing its power
B. Stores up electricity
C. Increases the power of a magnet

What is the voltage of the electricity supplied to your home?
A. 24 volts
B. 2,400 volts
C. 240 volts

Which scientist first discovered that wires carrying electricity have a magnetic field?
A. Hans Christian Oersted
B. Michael Faraday
C. Benjamin Franklin

...at do you call the parts of a magnet
...ere the magnetic effect is the
...ngest?
...Poles
...Ohms
...ines of force

...ich scientist invented the world's first
...tery?
...Benjamin Franklin
...Hans Christian Oersted
...Alessandre Volta

...at do you call the device for changing
...voltage of electricity?
...Transformer
...Volt meter
...Battery

...at is the name of the naturally magnetic
...k?
...Lodestone
...Amber
...ronside

...w much electricity can an electric eel
...duce?
...Less than 50 volts
...Up to 500 volts
...More than 5,000 volts

...at happens if you move a magnet
...ough a coil of wire?
...Electricity is generated in the wire
...lectricity is generated in the magnet
...Electricity is generated in the wire and the
...gnet

**How do migrating birds manage to find
their way on cloudy days?**
A. By using the Sun and stars
B. By wearing special glasses
C. By using the Earth's magnetic field as a
guide to help them navigate?

**What do hydroelectric power plants use to
generate electricity?**
A. Moving water
B. Burning fuel
C. Sunlight

Which of these has an electric charge?
A. Electrons
B. Protons
C. Both!

Answers:
B, B, A, B, B, A, C, A, A, C, A, A, C, B, A, B, A, C, A, C

Index

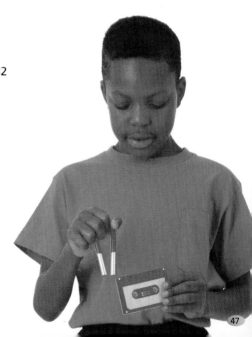

Published by
Two-Can Publishing
A Division of Zenith Entertainment plc
43–45 Dorset Street
London W1H 4AB

Author: Margaret Whalley
Consultants: Dr Christine Sutton, Ruth Bessant

First published by Two-Can Publishing in 2000
Copyright © Two-Can Publishing, 2000
Book text © Miranda Bower

Hardback ISBN 1-85434-776-4

Hardback 10 9 8 7 6 5 4 3 2 1

Photograph credits:
ZEFA: front cover;
Science Photo Library: p.11 (bottom right);
ZEFA: p.12 (top right), p.13 (bottom right),
p.20 (bottom left), p.32 (bottom left);
Science Photo Library: p.21 (top right), p.32 (top right);
Oxford Scientific Films: p.23 (centre right);
Science Photo Library/
European Space Agency: p.33 (centre right).

Illustrations by Nancy Anderson.

Reproduced by Next Century, Hong Kong
Printed by Wing King Tong, Hong Kong